**Know Your Bible** series

# WORKBOOK 2

**Psalm 103**
   **— a meditative study**

**Mark's Gospel**

**Love — a word study**

**Peter**

**Jeremiah**

**Human beings**
   **— warts and all!**

**Beginning the**
   **Pastoral Letters**

by Susan Penfold
Alistair Hornal
Ro Willoughby

**Inter-Varsity Press**

**Inter-Varsity Press**

38 De Montfort Street, Leicester LE1 7GP, England.

© Inter-Varsity Press, 1984

First published 1984

Reprinted 1984

British Library Cataloguing in Publication Data

Penfold, Susan
  Workbook 2.—(Know your Bible series; 2)
  1. Devotional calendars
  I. Title  II. Hornal, Alistair
  III. Willoughby, Ro  IV. Series
  242'.2    BS390

  ISBN 0-85110-723-0

Set in Helvetica, Palatino and Plantin

Typeset in Great Britain by Swanston Graphics Limited

Printed in Great Britain by
Hazell Watson & Viney Limited,
Member of the BPCC Group,
Aylesbury, Bucks

**Inter-Varsity Press is the publishing division of the Universities and Colleges Christian Fellowship (formerly the Inter-Varsity Fellowship), a student movement linking Christian Unions in universities and colleges throughout the United Kingdom and the Republic of Ireland, and a member movement of the International Fellowship of Evangelical Students. For information about local and national activities write to UCCF, 38 De Montfort Street, Leicester LE1 7GP.**

# Introduction

I praise God for publications such as the **Know Your Bible** series that encourage us to spend time in the Bible daily. As you use this well-written workbook, I trust you will discover the rich rewards that come from personally studying God's authoritative Word.

One cannot honestly study Scripture for long before sensing its tremendous authority. We do not find God offering mere suggestions but speaking authentic, powerful and true declarations about himself and ourselves, about history and eternity.

Yes, some still question the Bible's authority. But this isn't particularly new (see Genesis 3:1), nor should it be upsetting. Charles Spurgeon well said: 'Defend the Bible? Might as well defend a lion.' If God is God, then he could write a completely trustworthy book – and he did!

The study of God's authoritative Word has transformed my own life and ministry. Of course I read other books on theology, philosophy, history, psychology, and other areas of learning, and we should never stop learning and growing intellectually. But we have to come to the place where we accept God's Word over man's word.

Once you and I have settled the issue of God's authority over us, giving him the supremacy in our lives and studying his Word, then we can listen to others without being shaken. We can read what they have to say and weigh it intellectually and critically, because we judge everything they say in the light of Scripture:

*The Word of God is living and active. Sharper than any double-edged sword, it penetrates even to dividing soul and spirit, joints and marrow; it judges the thoughts and attitudes of the heart. Nothing in all creation is hidden from God's sight. Everything is uncovered and laid bare before the eyes of him to whom we must give account.* (Heb. 4:12-13, NIV)

I challenge you to let God revolutionize your thoughts and living as you use this workbook to study his Word.

**Luis Palau**

# How to use this book

**Encountering the living God on a daily basis is the most life-changing experience possible for any Christian. Confronted by God's standards and his view on life as we find them in the Bible, we either turn away from him or plead, in confidence, for him to change us and make us like Jesus.**

As you use these Bible studies, make it your overall aim to meet with God and become like him. If you have never had a regular time with God for study and prayer, you will find it helpful to use the guidelines on the back page.

We all need variety; we so easily get into a rut. So you'll find in this workbook different approaches to studying the Bible.

Basically, there are nine different types of study:

 Fairly detailed study of short consecutive passages in one book of the Bible.

 'Bird's-eye' study, taking long passages to get a broad view of a long book.

 Whole-book study, concentrating on major **themes** from a Bible book.

 Meditative study, where we dwell on one passage for several days, looking at it from different angles and letting its message really sink in.

 Word study, looking at key words in the Bible.

 History, getting the general flow of the story.

 Character study, showing how God dealt with an individual.

 Topics, outlining the Bible's teaching on particular aspects of the Christian life.

 Problem studies, pointing to what the Bible has to say on difficult or controversial issues.

We also need frameworks in which to work, and each series of studies has been designed to occupy **five daily sessions** of prayer and study of about **half an hour.** Then there are suggestions for **further study.**

The idea is to use the daily studies through the regular working week, Monday to Friday, and then weekends can be used for something slightly different, depending on whether you have more or less time.

We all have a pattern that works best for us, but do make sure you *have* a regular pattern. It's a good idea to jot down at the top of each study the day on which you do it.

And it isn't called a workbook for nothing! To get the most out of the series, you will need to have a notebook in which to record your discoveries. Don't be tempted just to 'do it in your head' — it's a great help to concentration and clear thinking if you actually write down your responses.

Nor is this meant to be just an academic exercise. A true understanding of the Bible affects our lives, so try hard to apply what you discover to your own life and the lives of those around you.

Many suggestions have been given to help you and it is most important to *pray* about what you have learnt. Having key Bible verses tucked in the corners of your memory will also help you to retain what you've discovered.

> *Bible study has torn apart my life and remade it. That is to say that God, through his Word, has done so. In the darkest periods of my life when everything seemed hopeless, I would struggle in the grey dawns of many faraway countries to grasp the basic truths of Scripture passages. I looked for no immediate answers to my problems. Only did I sense intuitively that I was drinking drafts from a fountain that gave life to my soul.*
>
> **John White,** *The Fight*

Built into the studies are a number of other symbols, suggesting the various activities involving you. You will soon get used to them! The key is as follows:

 Out with your notebook!

 Background information

 Branching out

 Pray

 Think

 Further reading

# Contents

# Psalm 103

Why should we praise God? The psalmist gives us many reasons here. As we look in some detail at what he says, it should encourage our own thanksgiving. Each study looks at just a few verses, but you should try to see where they fit into the whole psalm. Where cross references to other passages on a similar theme are given, don't feel obliged to look up all of them — concentrate on the psalm first, and use the other passages to help further reflection. You could also follow up other passages you know on a similar theme.

## 1 'Count your blessings'

### Psalm 103:1-5

The psalmist starts by encouraging himself to praise the Lord — with his whole being (verse 1), not merely an outward show. Like

8

him we probably need the command in verse 2 not to forget how much God has done for us — when we do remember, it should encourage us to praise God, just as it did him.

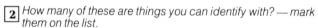

**1** *Look through the whole psalm and write a list of all the things the psalmist says the Lord has done for him.*

**2** *How many of these are things you can identify with? — mark them on the list.*

**3** *Now look back on your own experience as a Christian and write your own list of things (both spiritual and physical — see verse 3) for which you can praise the Lord.*

Now spend some time in praise and thanksgiving for yourself — use these lists to encourage you, as the psalmist did.

**Consider:** Can you honestly say with the psalmist 'He fills my life with good things' (verse 5)? — or are there things you do not yet have, and wish the Lord would give you? Now would be a good time to talk these over with God. It may be that these are blessings which God wants to give you at some time in the future, or it may be that God knows these things are not best for you (cf. Luke 11:9-13).

# Looking back 2

## Psalm 103:6-8

Not only can the psalmist look to his own experience of God's blessing to encourage his praise, but also that of the whole people of God down the ages and in his own time (notice the word 'our' and 'we' in verses 10,12,14). These verses recall the Lord's rescue of his people when they were oppressed in Egypt, and

particularly his covenant with them at Sinai, when he revealed himself and promised to guide them. Verse 7 recalls such verses as Exodus 33:12-17, and verse 8, Exodus 34:5-6.

**1** *What does the psalmist say here about God's character?*

Try to express it in different words from the psalm!

**2** *Consider: Can you think of examples of God's faithfulness to believers, either in past times, or in other parts of the world? Stop and thank God for his faithfulness, both to you and to others.*

*(Reading Christian biographies can be a great encouragement to your own faith in God, such as Dr Helen Roseveare's story, Give Me This Mountain (IVP, 1966), or Corrie ten Boom's The Hiding Place (Hodder, 1976).)*

As Christians we look back to Jesus' death and resurrection as the supreme revelation of God's love to us, just as the Jews looked back to the Exodus. **Read** Romans 8:31-39, where Paul uses this theme to encourage his readers to face their current problems. Why is it such a stimulus to confidence in God?

# 3 God's forgiveness

## Psalm 103:8-14

The psalmist turns to one particular example of God's compassion — his forgiveness.

**1** *How do we deserve to be treated (verse 10)?*

**2** *Why doesn't God treat us like that?*

Not an easy question! — the psalmist's only answer lies in his understanding of God's character — he uses poetic imagery to show how sure forgiveness is (verses 11-12). We have the privilege of seeing this much more clearly demonstrated in Jesus.

**Read:** 1 Peter 2:21-25. (Peter is making clear allusions to Isaiah 53 — you might like to read that as well).

**3** *What extra grounds do Christians have for being certain of God's forgiveness?*

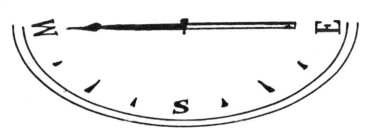

Stop and thank God for his forgiveness — it may help to remember specific sins from the last day or so, or even from further back, confess them, and thank God that they are so decisively put away (verse 12).

**4** *It is easy to take God's forgiveness too lightly! What attitude towards God does the psalmist expect in those who are forgiven? How will this affect our attitude towards sin?*

## 'We are dust' — **4**

### Psalm 103:13-18

**1** *What does the psalmist mean when he says we are dust (verse 14) and our life is like grass (verse 15)? (Do you ever think of yourself like this?)*

**2** *What does he say gives meaning to life?*

**3** *Think about your non-Christian friends. What is important to them? What do they use to give meaning to life?*

**Consider:** Do you ever let such things become more important to you than the Lord? Read Jesus' warning about such things in Matthew 6:19-24.

Read the whole psalm again, and look out for all that it says about the way the Lord loves us. Praise him for that love!

# 5 'Our God reigns'

## Psalm 103:17-22

As he contemplates all that God has done for him and for his people, the psalmist sums it up by saying that God rules over everything (verse 19).

1 *What response does the psalmist expect people to make to God's sovereignty?*

2 *Why do you think he calls not only men, but angels and all other creatures to join him in praise?*

3 *Read through the whole psalm again, and make a list of all that it teaches about God's character.*

**Consider:** What does the Lord's rule mean for you personally? Do you have any problems which seem to be insoluble? Are there areas of your life where what you want and what God wants don't coincide? As you think and pray about these, it may help to look back at what this psalm says about God's love and faithfulness.

### Weekend

**Pray:** Since God is king *over all* (verse 19), it follows that we can bring the needs of the whole world to him. Think of the major stories which have been in the news in the past week, and take time to pray for the needs which these represent. Try to understand something of the background to this week's crises, by careful reading of news reports and editorial comments. Do you know of Christian missions working in such areas, who could do with prayer now?

# Mark's Gospel

Traditionally the author of this Gospel is Mark, who appears at various times in the early days of the church. The reference of Mark 14:51 possibly applies to him. He may have been heavily influenced by Peter. This Gospel would therefore be a record of Peter's personal account of the life of Jesus.

This is the shortest Gospel and possibly the earliest. Matthew and Luke may have used it in writing their own accounts.

Mark may have been writing to Christians in Rome who were facing persecution under the Emperor Nero around AD 60-70. Encouragements to Christians in such a situation can be found throughout the Gospel.

Inevitably there will not be time to look at the Gospel in great detail, but this series will hopefully whet your appetitie! But above all pray that you will get to know Jesus better as a result of these studies. Allow him to rise out of the pages of this Gospel and speak to you.

Good commentaries for reference include the Tyndale Commentary on Mark by R. A. Cole (IVP), The Gospel of Mark, by William Lane (the New International Commentary, Paternoster) and Ralph P. Martin, Where the Action Is (Gospel Light).

## The opening section

1

## Mark 1:1-13

### Structure

These verses are often described as 'the Prologue to Mark's Gospel'. Here he presents the central figure of his account,

Jesus. He did not want anyone to be in doubt about whom he was writing.

**Interest point**

The common theme running through the opening section is that of the wilderness. It is a theme that recurs throughout the Gospel. For any Jewish reader the wilderness or desert stood for a number of things:

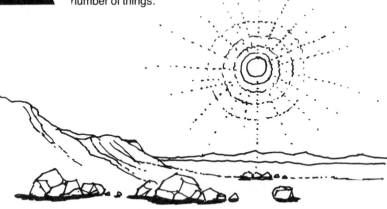

- a time of testing and failure after they had left Egypt,
- a time when they were called to repentance,
- a time when God appeared to them in a new way and when he gave them the law as a sign that they were in a special relationship with him,
- a time when they knew his care for and guidance of them, and it was anticipated that when the Messiah came, he would gather the redeemed to him in the wilderness.

1 *As you read the Gospel, look out for the wilderness or desert symbolism. Which of the ideas associated with the wilderness do you find present in the opening section?*

2 *Repentance was central not only to John's message but also to that of Jesus. What did John say about it? In your own words write down what else you understand by the word. You could ask other Christian friends what they mean by it as well and look up 'repentance' in a concordance.*

3 *What is Mark saying about the central figure of his Gospel in this opening section?*

What was John's attitude to Jesus? He has been described as the first preacher of the good news of Christ. What is your attitude to Jesus when you are telling others about him? Do you start with what you think about him, so that it ends up with Jesus being almost obscured by you and your experiences? What can you do to prevent this happening?

# The first phase of the Galilean ministry

2

## Mark 1:14-45

**Structure**

Mark records a similar pattern at the start of the early phase of the ministry to that of the later phase. Both phases start with Jesus' activity (1:14-15; *cf.* 3:7-12), followed by the call of the apostles (1:16-20; *cf.* 3:13-19).

**Interest point**

The ordinary people addressed Jesus as 'Lord' (7:28), 'Teacher' (9:17), 'Son of David' (10:47-48), 'Master' (10:51). But demoniacs called him 'the Holy One of God' (1:24), 'Son of God' (3:11), 'Son of the Most High God' (5:7). The demons had superior knowledge of Jesus' identity. They were not acknowledging him as God but as a defensive action were trying to call him to order — they failed!

I   *Right from the start the characteristics of the new kingdom or order brought in by Jesus were apparent — both by what he said and by what he did. Note down how you think Jesus' actions here demonstrated its coming.*

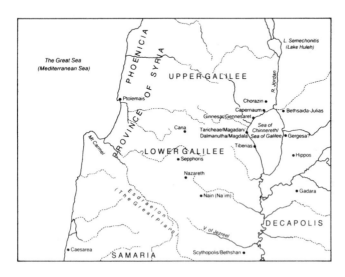

**2** *It was impossible not to react in some way to Jesus. Contrast the reactions of the following groups. Why did they react as they did?*

- *the disciples*
- *the evil spirits*
- *the sick*

By his words and actions Jesus commanded obedience. Can you think of any time recently when he called you to an act of obedience? What was your reaction?

# 3 The first phase, continued

Mark 2:1 – 3:6

### Structure
These Galilean controversies could be said to be balanced by the five Jerusalem ones in 11:27 – 12:37.

### Interest point
The term 'the Son of man' appears twice in this chapter. Then it is only after Peter acknowledges Jesus as the Messiah in 8:29 that Mark uses it again, twelve times, as Jesus discloses his identity to his disciples alone. The phrase may simply have been a substitute that Jesus used for 'I', but at times it possibly had some Messianic connotations (*e.g.* 14:62). Jesus may have had in mind Daniel's marvellous vision (Daniel 7:9 -14) in using the phrase.

**1** *Read the passage and then pin-point what issue was at stake in each of the five controversies. (2:1-12; 2:13-17; 2:18-22; 2:23-28; 3:1-6). Then beside each point note down*

*Jesus' response to the controversy. What did you discover
about the character of Jesus and how he viewed his mission?*

**2** *His claims about himself are stunning in their original context.
How challenging do you honestly believe the good news of
Jesus is to your own situation? Take each of the five
responses and try to apply them to your own circumstances.*

**3** *What could the offer of forgiveness mean to those you know
whose lives are broken and guilt-ridden?*

**4** *What about those who lead good lives, acknowledging their
own high moral code, but who do not have any time for God?*

Pray for those of whom you have been reminded as you have
considered these five controversies.

# Later in the Galilean ministry

# 4

## Mark 3:7-35; 6:1-13

### Structure
As with the earlier phase, this starts with a summary of Jesus'
activity followed by the commissioning of the disciples.

## Interest point

The idea of rejection occurs throughout this section — those who refuse to accept Jesus and his miracles or who fail to understand him do so because of their hardness of heart. Already in 3:6 the opposition is wanting to kill him.

**1** *Draw out the similarities in 3:13-18 and 6:6b-13 from the two callings of the disciples. How did Jesus call them and to what ? Notice that he first called them to be **with** him. There is a danger that action in serving God can come before spending time with him. How can you safeguard yourself from this? Pray for any you know who are in danger of being so busy serving God that he is actually being squeezed out of their lives.*

**2** *Jesus faced rejection from many sources. Why did the following reject him? — members of his family, the teachers of the law, the people of Nazareth, some of those who heard the disciples.*

Jesus came to bring salvation in the face of rejection and hostility — from men and from Satan himself. His disciples too had to face similar rejection. In what ways have you been misunderstood or rejected because of your faith? What reassurance can you find in these verses?

# 5 Later in the Galilean ministry, continued

## Mark 4:1-34

### Structure
This is the largest grouping of Jesus' parables by Mark. All three parables illustrate the character of the coming of the kingdom of God.

### Interest point: the kingdom of God

The phrase 'the kingdom of God' stands for God's reign of salvation and righteousness at the end of time. This cosmic saving rule of God began in the ministry of Christ, and was strengthened by his death and resurrection, and the pouring out of the Spirit. It will finally be consummated in the end of the world and the re-creation of the universe. Thus the kingdom of God has begun and is with us now, yet not completely.

*In the first parable (4:1-20) notice that the sower and the seed are presented as being good and the climax of the story is the good harvest rather than the attempts of the poorer soils to produce a harvest. In your own words, what sort of responses to the seed are characterized here? Can you think of any of your friends who have responded to the word of God in a similar way to one of the soils? Pray for them now, that they will become more receptive to the truth, or praise God for them if they are already bearing fruit.*

Jesus was urging his hearers to listen carefully and act responsibly to his words (21-25). Yet on the other hand it would appear in the parable of the growing seed (26-29) and the mustard seed (30-32) that man's part in the bringing in of the kingdom is non-existent. What was Jesus saying about the kingdom of God in these two parables? How would it come and what would it be like? List some of its features. What does this say about the ways in which God chooses to work?

**Weekend**
Look up the following references to Jesus' rejection and suffering which are found later in the Gospel: 5:17; 8:31 – 9:1; 9:12-13, 30-32; 10:32-34,45; 11:18; 12:1-12. If you have time, read the account of the crucifixion in chapters 14 and 15 as well.

# Mark's Gospel, continued

## 1 ) Later in the Galilean ministry, continued

### Mark 4:35 – 5:43

**Interest point**

A common theme in Mark is that, although Jesus spent much time with the disciples, they often misunderstood and he had to rebuke them, 4:40 is just one example. See also 7:18; 8:17-18,21,32-33; 9:19.

In these four miracles Mark wrote of the power of Jesus at work over nature, the forces of evil, death and chronic sickness.

**1** *If you were reading these verses for the first time, what would strike you about Jesus? Write down your observations.*

**2** *Pin-point the reactions of the disciples, the demon-possessed man, the people in the Decapolis, Jairus and the woman with the bleeding, to such demonstrations of Jesus' power. How do they give both good and bad examples about faith and the need to respond to Jesus and what he has done?*

Write down some things that Jesus has done for you, *e.g.* in saving you from sin, and in removing fear. How have you reacted to what he's done? Then thank him and pray that you may grow in responsive faith and in obedience.

# Withdrawal beyond Galilee

## Mark 6:14-56

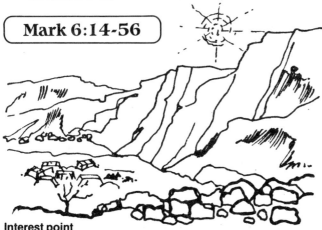

**Interest point**

The New Testament writers relied heavily on their Jewish background in writing, frequently finding parallels between the Old Testament era and the new era brought in by Jesus. One example is here, where Mark could be paralleling John the Baptist with Elijah, and possibly Herod and Herodias with Ahab and Jezebel (1 Kings 19:1-2). The wilderness motif is another example which is brought out in these verses. The feeding of the 5,000 could be paralleled with Israel in the wilderness, experiencing the compassion of God who feeds and teaches them (Exodus 16:4-16; Deuteronomy 29:2-6). Notice also the phrase of Jesus in 6:34, 'sheep without a shepherd', which is also used by Moses in Numbers 27:17.

**1** *The ministry of Jesus aroused Herod's conscience. What had been his attitude and behaviour towards John while he was alive (verse 20)? Yet he remained untouched by John's message. Can you think of examples of people today whose conscience can be aroused by hearing about Jesus and the truth about him and yet remain untouched? Pray for them and for any Christians who are in regular contact with them.*

**2** *The love and compassion of Jesus are outstanding. In what ways was his love demonstrated in these two miracles — towards both the crowds and his disciples? Note down your comments.*

Recently, how have you experienced his love towards you? How far are you willing to allow his compassion to flow through you towards others? (Don't pass quickly over this question!)

# 3 Withdrawal beyond Galilee, continued

## Mark 7:1-37

### Structure
7:1-23 forms a single teaching unit which seems to have no clear relation to what has gone before nor what follows after it. Fitted in here, however, it forms a prelude to the three miracle narratives in which Jesus extends his grace to the Gentiles. The unit's position is similar in structure to the place of the teaching unit (4:1-34) in the period of Jesus' later Galilean ministry (3:7 – 6:8).

**1** *What was wrong with the Pharisees' view of the law and tradition and what did that mean in practice? How had this affected their views towards the attitude of the heart?*

**2** *Note — the law itself was not wrong; it was given by God and written down. Rather, Jesus was calling into question the authority of the oral law of tradition accumulated over the centuries.*

**3** *How easy is it to be bound by traditions or customs of the church or Christian group to which you belong — so that they become more important than God himself? Is this so in patterns of worship, or the way that you spend Sunday?*

**4** *So what, then, is Jesus saying to those who keep the letter of the law without the spirit of it?*

### Note of verses 26-30
At first sight, it looks as if Jesus is insensitive to the Gentile woman with her crying need. Is Jesus out of character here?

The faith of the Gentile woman and of the deaf man with his friends provides a sharp contrast to the behaviour of the Pharisees, crowd and the disciples. Write down all the contrasts you can see in their attitudes and behaviour. You might find it useful to make two columns.

# Withdrawal beyond Galilee, continued

## 4

### Mark 8:1-30

**Structure**

In 6:31 – 7:37 Mark has presented a pattern of incidents which includes a feeding of a multitude, encountering the unbelief of religious leaders and acts of healing. 8:1-30 has a similar pattern, climaxing in the confession of 8:27-30. The first pattern ends with the deaf ears of the man being opened. The second pattern ends with the deaf ears and the blind eyes of the disciples being opened.

**Interest point**

The conversation at Caesarea Philippi (8:27-30) is the climax of the preceding chapters. Up to now, Mark has made no clear statement about Jesus' identity except in 1:1. From this point he shows Jesus talking openly about his death. He has set his face towards Jerusalem. This dominates the rest of the Gospel.

**1** *The disciples could hardly have forgotten about the previous feeding of the 5,000, yet they seemed unsure of what Jesus would do (8:4). Their lack of faith, however, was different from the blatant unbelief of the Pharisees. From verses 1-21 what differences can you detect?*

**2** *The unbelief of the Pharisees meant that they wanted to judge him on their own terms: 'Give us a sign'. What was Jesus' response to them? Ask God to forgive you if at any time you have made demands on him and judged him when to do so is like throwing an insult in his face.*
*Note — 'yeast' was a common metaphor for corruption.*

If someone were to ask you what you thought about Jesus, what would you say (without using any jargon)? Write down your answer. What about getting a friend to read it and talk about it with you?

# 5 Journey to Jerusalem

## Mark 8:31 — 9:50

### Structure
In this section Mark records three times Jesus' explanation of his death to his disciples (8:31; 9:31; 10:33) and each time it is followed by misunderstanding and then teaching by Jesus on the nature of true discipleship.

1 *In your own words, summarize what Jesus said and taught in the first two declarations about his death and then about the subsequent call to discipleship — 8:31 – 9:1 and 9:31-50. You will need to write down your summary.*

2 *Putting the interests of God and others before your own is never easy. In practical terms, what does this mean to you? From these verses what motivates you to live by this standard?*

3 *In what ways could the transfiguration (9:2-13) have helped the disciples to understand Jesus' identity, forthcoming death and glorification?*

As you read verses 14-29 try to enter into the weary exasperation of Jesus towards his disciples and their misunderstanding. And yet he did not give up on them. Do you think that Jesus is often exasperated with you and your slowness of heart? Spend time thinking over this and praise God that he has not deserted you.

### Weekend
1 *Look back on your notes. Some of the studies may have taken longer than you expected or had time for. But above all, remind yourself of what you have learnt about Jesus.*

2 *Pick out one incident from Jesus' life that has particularly struck you this week. Now tell it in your own words from the point of view of one of the people involved (it could even be Christ's!)*

# Mark's Gospel, continued

## Journey to Jerusalem, continued

# 1

## Mark 10:1-52

Read verses 1-12.

Jesus' purpose in explaining the Mosaic law on divorce (Deuteronomy 24:1) in verse 5 was to restate that divorce was not acceptable but may be necessary to limit sinfulness and control its consequences, a direct response to the question of verse 2. God's pattern was, and has always been, that of a lasting partnership between a man and a woman. In the subsequent discussion with the disciples he put man and woman on the same level in marriage — which was truly shocking for his time.

**1** *What does this indicate about God's intentions for human beings which are so often higher and better than our way of doing things?*

**2** *Can you think of other examples?*

**3** *Pray that you will always strive to let God mould your ideas.*

**4** *God does not always give to people what they ask of him. Blind Bartimaeus got what he asked for, but the rich young ruler went away sad. Read verses 17-23 and 46-52. What do we see here about the way that Jesus granted requests which people made of him? In what attitude of mind do you ask God for things?*

To complete the observations you made in the last study about the statement of Jesus' death and the call to discipleship, look at verses 24-45. Jot down what these add to your understanding.

# 2 Ministry in Jerusalem

## Mark 11:1 – 12:44

### Structure
This section is divided into two: 11:1-25 consists of the symbolic actions accomplished during the three days in Jerusalem, and 11:27 – 12:44 the five conflicts with priestly and scribal authorities (possibly paralleled with the Galilean ones, 2:1 – 3:6).

### Interest point
In fulfilment of Zechariah 9:9 Jesus was coming as Messiah into Jerusalem, coming as Lord to his temple, although the disciples did not understand the significance until afterwards (John 12:16). It was unlikely that Jesus wanted his action to be understood as a claim to political messiahship. The cursing of the fig tree could be seen as another Messianic act, since the fig tree often symbolized Israel's status before God (*e.g.* Jeremiah 8:13) and its destruction was associated with judgment (*e.g.* Hosea 2:12). In cleansing the temple forecourt Jesus was symbolically enabling the Gentiles to worship God — a fulfilment of Zechariah 14:16.

1 *As you read 11:1-25, make a note of all the indications that Jesus was always in control of events and not vice versa. What grounds for praise does that give you?*

2 *Briefly summarize the criticisms levelled at Jesus in 11:27 – 12:44. How did he handle such criticism? What hints can you get from him on how you can confront those who criticize you for your faith? When, if ever, are you entitled to attack such critics in the devastating way that Jesus did?*

Praise God that even in the face of such opposition Jesus remained firm, refusing to act in any way other than might be expected of God-become-man.

## Mark 13:1-37

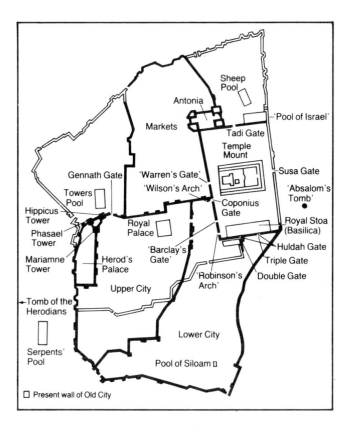

**Structure**

This is the longest uninterrupted discourse of Jesus in Mark's Gospel. It provides a bridge between Jesus' public ministry and the account of his death, showing a link between the judgment of Jerusalem and the death of Jesus (see 14:58; 15:29).

**Interest point**

The primary function of chapter 13 is not to predict details of future events but to promote faith and obedience in a time of distress and upheaval. This would be particularly relevant to the original

27

readers undergoing persecution. As you can imagine, much scholarly debate has been focused upon the chapter. Was Jesus referring to the fall of Jerusalem in AD 70, or to his second coming, or what? In this study we shall not attempt to answer such questions!

**1** *What were the motives of Jesus in instructing the disciples on how they were to view the future? Consider each of the following statements to see which of them gives a clue as to his motives. Note down which verse(s), if any, applies to which statement.*

*Jesus taught his disciples about the future because...*

- *he wanted them to be prepared for whatever happened.*
- *he did not want them to be deceived.*
- *he wanted them to be confident in the face of persecution.*
- *he wanted to motivate them to preach.*
- *he wanted them to take a long holiday every winter.*
- *he wanted to increase their trust in the sovereignty of God.*
- *he wanted them to spend all their lives analysing the signs of the times.*

**2** *Take each of the above **relevant** statements and prayerfully consider how you yourself are taking the teaching of Jesus to heart.*

# 4 The road to death

## Mark 14:1-52

**Structure**

So many of Mark's themes are down together in what is obviously the climax of his Gospel: for example, the conflict with the authorities, the plans to kill Jesus, the awareness that Jesus has had all along of his mission and impending death and the ways in which he prepared his disciples for it. Mark was preparing his readers for this moment, for the passion of Jesus.

> 'He was despised and rejected by men,
>   a man of sorrows, and familiar with suffering.
> Like one from whom men hide their faces
>   he was despised, and we esteemed him not'
>                                   (Isaiah 53:3).

As you read these verses, bear this prophecy about the Messiah in mind. Make a note of all the different ways in which Jesus was rejected. His loneliness and isolation were finally tragically expressed in his cry from the cross in 15:34. What does such utter desolation mean? Then pause to realize that he went to such depths for you. In humility praise God that Jesus was obedient, even to the point of death on the cross.

*My God, my God, why have you forsaken me?*

Even at this late stage, what was Jesus saying to his disciples about the purpose of his suffering? How would you answer someone who said to you that the death of Jesus was a tragedy because it was a pointless death of the best man who ever lived? Use this passage to help you in your answer.

# The road to death, continued
# 5

## Mark 14:53 – 15:47

'He was oppressed and afflicted,
   yet he did not open his mouth;
he was led like a lamb to the slaughter,
   and as a sheep before her shearers is silent,
   so he did not open his mouth'
   (Isaiah 53:7).

1 | *Familiarity can blunt our senses. As you read this moving and well-known narrative, bear this prophecy of Isaiah in mind. Notice the indignity of the Son of God, who had left all the glories of heaven to come to this earth, yet being treated in this way. What right had any man to do that to Jesus? You may feel anger welling up inside you. Allow yourself to respond to God in a way that seems appropriate.*

**2** *As in his life, so in his death, the person of Jesus provoked a reaction. How would you describe the reactions of the following?*

- *anyone in the temple at the time when the curtain split*
- *the centurion*
- *the woman*
- *Joseph*
- *Pilate*

*No-one can be indifferent to Jesus when they meet him.*

**Interest point,** verse 38
The curtain separated the Holy of Holies, where God was believed to be present in a special way, from the rest of the temple. The high priest went in there only once every year. Now, by the death of Jesus, access to God was available to everyone.

**Structure**
The statement about Jesus, with which Mark begins his Gospel, is now to be found upon the lips of a non-Jew, at the end of the Gospel. 'Surely this man was the Son of God' (verse 39).

---

**Weekend**

# The resurrection of Jesus

## 16:1-20

**1** *Read 16:1-8 (many authorities believe verses 9-20 are a later addition to the Gospel). The tragedy gave way to triumph, as Jesus had predicted (**e.g.**10:34; 14:28). If he had not been resurrected he would, among other things, have been a liar. From your own knowledge and looking at these verses and· 1 Corinthians 15:12-34, why is it important that the cross was not the end for Jesus?*

**2** *Spend some time over the weekend reviewing your studies in this Gospel. But above all, ask yourself how much have you discovered about Jesus and in what ways has he met you and spoken to you over these last three weeks?*

**Further reading**

**3** *The resurrection of Jesus provides a solid historical basis for Christianity's claim to be true. It is examined thoroughly in **Jesus Christ: The Witness of History**, by J.N.D. Anderson (IVP) and **Who Moved the Stone?**, by Frank Morison (STL).*

# Love

It would be very difficult to talk about the Christian gospel without mentioning love. But what is it? The word 'love' conjures up all sorts of ideas. We shall look at how the concept comes across in the Bible itself.

## ◁ Love is... 1

### 1 Corinthians 13

The church at Corinth had a lot going for it. But it had problems! Not the least of these involved divisions into various party groups and irregularities in worship.

The Church had written to the apostle Paul about these and other issues, and time and again he hints at love as being the solution to their problems.

Chapter 13 focuses the reader's attention directly on love — its meaning and importance.

31

**1** *How would you define what love is? Before reading the passage, write down your definition and then test it against verses 4-7. Can you think of any other ways of briefly summarizing the meaning of love, or of other words you could use in its place?*

**2** *In verses 1-3 you will read some startling statements. Why, do you think, should lack of love make these apparently highly spiritual activities worthless?*

**3** *Verses 8-13 contrast temporary things with the permanence of faith, hope and love. How do Paul's pictures about growing up and mirrors (vv.11-12) help you to see the importance of faith, hope and love over 'temporary' things?*

Notice the supremacy of love over even faith and hope (verse 13). Pray about what you plan to do today and ask God to help you to 'make love your aim' (14:1) in everything you do and say.

# 2 Loving and being loved ▷

## 1 John 4:7-12

*agapē*

The characteristic word for love in the New Testament is *agapē*. It was not used widely in Greek-speaking society, but was picked up by Christians to bring out the special quality of love that God has for us — and that we should have for him and for other people.

John addresses his readers as *agapētoi* — those who are especially loved. (The translation 'Dear friends' is a weak substitute for the old-fashioned word 'beloved'. In its singular form — *agapētos* — it is the word used by God the Father to describe his special love for his 'beloved' Son, *e.g.* in Matthew 3:17.)

As people whom God especially loves we have special responsibilities.

**1** *'Without love — nothing!' How does this principle from 1 Corinthians 13 work out in 1 John 4:7-8? Why can you not be a Christian without having love?*

**2** *Where did your love relationship with God begin (verse 10)? How can you be sure that God still loves you? (Before you write down your answer, compare verse 9 with John 3:16; Romans 5:8; then read Romans 5:6-11.)*

**3** *If God's love is seen through his actions in your favour, how should you love other people (verses 11-12)? What unseen resources can you draw on to enable you to love like God?*

**4** *How can you be confident that God will not stop loving you? (Think again about what you read in Romans 5.)*

(As 1 John 4:8 says that 'God is love', you may like to substitute 'God' for 'love' in 1 Corinthians 13, and then use these verses to help you worship God.)

# Love that lasts

**3**

## Deuteronomy 7:6-11

One of the great Old Testament words for love is *hesed* (often translated as 'steadfast/constant love', 'loving-kindness' or even 'mercy'). It focuses on the permanence of the relationship that God has with his people to whom he has committed himself.

In Genesis, God promised Abraham that he would be his God and the God of his descendants, and he sealed this covenant commitment with an oath (Genesis 15:18-20; 17:1-8).

God's love involves commitment: steadfast love.

In Deuteronomy 7, set just before Israel takes possession of the promised land, God restates this covenant relationship.

**1** *Why did God choose Israel (verses 6-7)? Write your answer in terms of (a) motive and (b) purpose. Make a special note of any reasons that clearly are not grounds for God's choice.*

**2** *How was God's love seen in action on Israel's behalf (verse 8)? Note any parallels between this and how God's love for you was displayed. (See your notes on Study 2).*

**3** *In the last study you saw that your love relationship with God began with God rather than with you. But love is not all one way. How is this brought out in verses 9-10?*

Study 5 will pick up the relationship of 'love' to 'law'. Begin to think about how God's love is seen in his action towards us and note any ways in which you can show your love for him in the light of verse 11.

# 4 God loves you!

## John 3:16; Ephesians 5:25-27; Romans 8:28-39

1 *What does John 3:16 tell you about the extent of God's love — and the conditions of benefiting from it?*

2 *Ephesians 5:25-27 pictures Christ's love for the church in terms of a bridegroom's love for his bride. (This parallels the Old Testament picture of God's covenant love for Israel as his bride.) In your own words, write down what Jesus wants to do to express his love to you as a Christian, based on this passage.*

*Read Romans 8:28-39. List what this passage teaches you about the results of (a) your love for God, and (b) God's love for you. Why can the apostle write with such certainty (verse 32)?*

**3** *Many people encounter difficulties over the Bible's teaching concerning election: how does God's special love for some square with his love for all the world?*

*The idea of choosing a bride can be a helpful one in appreciating what God has done: that God has chosen a special people for himself — as you saw he did with Israel in the last Study.*

The fact of God's undeserved and electing love must not be allowed to detract from God's loving offer of life to all who will believe in Jesus.

**4** *Think over Romans 8:29-30. Try to grasp the idea of a love which stretches from eternity to eternity — beginning in God's foreknowledge (which means much the same as his 'forelove') and ending in glorification for Christians.*

Rededicate yourself to Christ in readiness for the church's presentation as his bride (Ephesians 5:27-29).

# 'Do you love me?' 5

## John 21:15-17

*This is an encounter between Peter and Jesus after his resurrection. Three times Jesus asks his friend, 'Do you love me?', and he then gives Peter a threefold commission to look after his sheep. This must have brought great reassurance to the disciple who had denied his Lord three times.*

Two Greek words for love are used in this dialogue: *agapē* and *phileō*. Much ink has been spilt over why these different words are used. It could be that a contrast is intended between different qualities of love. (*Phileō* may be understood as 'tender affection' or 'friendship'.) But the distinction cannot be clearly determined — and it is reasonable to assume that John is just using different words for variety.

*phileō and agapē*

**1** *Read John 14:15-24 (part of what Jesus said to his disciples on the night he was betrayed). How do Jesus' words help you to know if your love for him is genuine? (NB verses 15,21,23 and 24.) Write your response after looking at Jesus' own example in verse 31.*

**2** *Refer to Matthew 22:35-40. Jesus is teaching that all the commands of the law — i.e. everything that God requires of us — hang on the twin cord of love for God and love for your neighbour. How does this reflect what Jesus says in John·14?*

**3** *Does this link between love and obedience help you to answer for yourself the question Jesus put to Peter in John 21?*

If you have time, go back over 1 Corinthians 13:4-7 and read your own name in the place of 'love'. Ask God for grace to make that ring true.

### Weekend

**1** *The word 'love' covers a number of quite distinct concepts. C. S. Lewis's book **The Four Loves** (Fontana) would make interesting weekend reading if you want to follow this up.*

erōs

**2** *The idea of **erōs** — the love that aims to possess, or sexual love — does not appear explicitly in the New Testament. However, the Old Testament provides many examples of love used in this and other senses. You can check this out under 'love' in an analytical concordance. Try to work out for yourself what the Hebrew words 'āhēḇ, dôḏ and ra'yâ mean.*

**3** *Song of Solomon is a beautiful poem about human love. You may like to read it and note in your notebook some of the lessons you learn.*

**4** *Alternatively, you may like to read Hosea's love story (Hosea 1-3), which is not only a tragic tale of human love, but a picture of God's love and the response to it.*

# Peter

## Peter, the fisherman

**1**

### Luke 5:1-11; John 1:35-42

Just suppose that you have been asked to write a biography of Peter. The only source material that you have to work with is to be found in the New Testament. Throughout the week, make a list of all the biographical details you might want to include — his background, activities, attitudes, relationships and any changes you detect in him over the years.

You could also asterisk any characteristics that you share with him. How did God deal with him? Might he treat you in the same way?

**1** *Begin by reading these two passages and listing the biographical details you discover. In what ways do you see yourself in Peter?*

**2** *Peter followed Jesus voluntarily. But how had Jesus demonstrated that he was greater than Peter and worth following? In your own words, how did Peter respond to Jesus' authority?*

**3** *Can you think of any who have such a limited view of Jesus, that they don't see the point in following him? How can you help them to see Jesus as he really is? (It may be that they are so proud and so blind that they are unable to recognize something of his greatness.) Pause to pray for them now.*

In Peter's experience, he first needed to recognize who Jesus was, limited though that recognition may be. It was then that Jesus gave him the commission to follow him. How far has that been the pattern you can trace in your own life, when you became a Christian and subsequently in your Christian life?

# 2 Peter, jumped in feet first

## Matthew 14: 22-33; 16:13-23; 26:31-35, 69-75

> You are the Christ, the Son of the living God

Each of these incidents will give you more information for your biography. Note down additional details of Peter's character. Asterisk those characteristics you share with him.

1. *In your own words summarize how Jesus dealt with Peter on each of these occasions. Was Jesus treating him consistently?*

2. *Peter was always a man for action and speaking his mind. At times this was a good thing, but at other times his forwardness led to sin. Recently, when have you been able to speak out for God or acted boldly and God has used you? Praise God that he has used you.*

3. *On the other hand, when have you spoken or acted impetuously and without thought? You may not be reduced to the bitter tears which Peter shed, but pause to ask for God's forgiveness and an openness for him to reveal himself to you as he did to Peter (Matthew 16:17).*

# Peter, with a job still to do

## 3

John 21

After reading this chapter, note the additional material you find there about Peter's life. In what ways can you identify with him? Also, look back to Week 5, Study 5, on love (page 35).

Peter's denial of Jesus must have made a very deep mark on him. His bitter tears of regret and failure were not crocodile tears! But by this time, overjoyed that Jesus was alive again, he with the other disciples were in a period of waiting. But they hardly knew what they were waiting for. It would be quite natural, though, for them to go off on a fishing expedition.

1  *Why was this conversation between Jesus and Peter so crucially important? What does it suggest about Jesus' attitude to failure and the way in which Peter himself responded to his failure? Is there any sense in which you have failed God and need to assure him of your love for him and willingness to serve him despite your failures? (Don't manufacture a failure for the sake of it!)*

2  *Have you known a time of uncertainty and waiting, possibly following a time of humiliation, emotional turmoil? Have you anguished over the need to make a decision about the future? What reassurance can you find from Jesus' conversation with Peter that God does not abandon those whom he loves, whom he intends to use in the future? If you are in such a period at the moment, pray for yourself in the light of what you have read and for any others that you know in such a situation.*

# 4 · Peter, filled with the Spirit

## Acts 4:1-22

By this stage there are definite signs that Peter was being changed, although he continued to make blunders throughout his life.

Read this section and note down any further information about Peter. The background of this passage is found in Acts 3.

**1** *Compare Peter here with Peter as we read about him in Matthew 26. How do you account for the difference? Acts 4:8 should give you one clue.*

**2** *The Holy Spirit strengthened Peter for a particular situation when clarity of speech and boldness were essential. He was experiencing in practice the promise of Jesus in Mark 13:11. Pray for any you know who are involved in the work of spreading the gospel and speaking in hostile environments, that they may learn to rely on God to give them the right words to say. You ought to include yourself in this!*

**3** *You may not have identified yourself with Peter today, apart perhaps from seeing yourself as ordinary (verse 13)! But Peter made the most of the opportunity which was presented to him. How can you look out **today** for similar opportunities, although they may be of a less dramatic nature?*

For Peter such an attitude involved considerable discomfort. How prepared are you for that? (At the end of the day, think about how you have used the last 24 hours to speak out for Jesus and to show him to others by the quality of your life. Have people been able to see that *you* have been a companion of Jesus?)

# Peter, feeding the sheep 5

## 1 Peter 1:1-2; 5:1-14

Towards the end of his life, Peter wrote at least two letters to isolated groups of Christians, obeying the command of Jesus to be a shepherd to the sheep. He had some strong things to say to them, but his deep concern for his fellow Christians is very evident. If you had time you would enjoy reading the whole letter. However, start by reading these two extracts.

**1** *What insights do they give into his character?*

**2** *List the encouragements and instructions that he gives to his fellow Christians, especially the leaders.*

**3** *His care for them is demonstrated by the high standards that he sets. Unlike Peter you are probably not in a position to give such instructions to many other Christians, but think of your Christian friends. What are your ambitions for them? Do you long for them to apply Peter's guidance to their own lives? Putting Peter's instructions into your own words, turn them into prayer bearing your friends in mind.*

**4** *Peter has a special concern for his fellow elders, reminding them of their responsibilities. Pray for the leaders of your church, that they will be able to live up to the standards God requires of them.*

It is easy for leaders to become discouraged. Can you think of some way in which you can encourage one of the leaders in your church, this week?

**Over the weekend...**
*You could look up all the references to Peter in a concordance. But do find time to look over your notes on what you have studied this week, noting especially the way in which God took Peter as he was, enthusiastic, outspoken and dominant, and used him, refined him and made him like Jesus.*

*We have not had time to read about Peter's contribution to the growth of the early church. You could do that on your own! Look at, for example, Acts 1:15-26; 2:14 – 3:26; 5:12-42; 10; 12:1-19.*

# Jeremiah

*P.S.*

Jeremiah was called to be a prophet — someone who spoke God's word at a time when his country, Judah, was relatively prosperous. However, during the forty or so years of his career he saw all that change, and he had the unenviable task of warning the people that God's judgment was going to come in a series of disasters, culminating in the destruction of Jerusalem. The book gives us much of his preaching, and also accounts of what happened to the prophet, and his reactions to the events taking place around him.

The book of Jeremiah can seem confusing, as some of it is arranged topically and some chronologically. Broadly speaking chapters 1-25 are messages from the Lord for Judah and her rulers; 26-45 are events in Jeremiah's life, probably recorded by his secretary, Baruch; 46-51 are prophecies against other nations; and chapter 52 is a postscript describing the fall of Jerusalem.

## 1 > The prophet's call

### Jeremiah 1

**Read** the chapter (preferably more than once), looking out for details of the job Jeremiah was being given.

1:1-3 is the heading of the book, summarizing the extent of Jeremiah's career. Take a sheet of paper and start a time-chart (to which you can add other dates as we go along), so you will be able to see how the events of Jeremiah's life fit together. The 13th year of Josiah's reign was 627 BC and he died in 608 BC. Jehoiakim was king until 597 BC, and the people were taken into exile (verse 3) in 587 BC. (NB — There were two other kings during this time, but they reigned for only three months each — more on this in Study 5.)

The rest of the chapter tells of the events which made Jeremiah realize the Lord was calling him to be a prophet.

1 *What can you find out about Jeremiah's character?*

2 *In what ways does God equip him for his job? What reassurance does he give Jeremiah that he can accomplish the job he is being called to do?*

3 *How do you think the visions (verses 11-16) helped Jeremiah to understand his job better?*

**Note:** *Verses 11-12.* The Hebrew has a play on words — the word for 'almond' sounds like the word for 'watching'.

*almond*

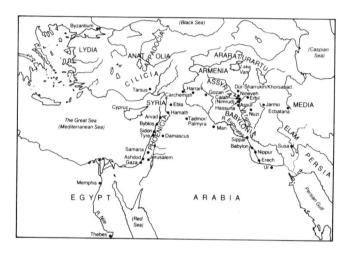

*Assyria and Babylon*

**Consider:** Jeremiah was reluctant to accept God's call. Was his reluctance justified? Have you ever been in the position of not wanting to do what God has asked you to? What help can you find here for such a situation?

# National renewal?

2

2 Kings 22:1-20; 23:1-4,21-30

When Josiah became king things in Judah were in a sorry state — idol worship and social injustice were common. No doubt this was partly an attempt to win favour with their foreign oppressors, Assyria, by worshipping their gods as well as the Lord. However Assyria was no longer powerful, and Josiah was able to take steps to put things right.

22:3 Mark 18th year on your time-chart

The book which was found in the temple was probably Deuteronomy, or the bulk of it.

**1** *What practical steps did Josiah take to implement its teaching? (The verses omitted, 23:5-20, contain a detailed description of the destruction of idol worship.)*

**2** *What does the passage say about the results of disobeying God?*

**3** *What are the results of obeying God for Josiah?*

23:26 Manasseh - Josiah's grandfather, an idolator

**4** *In what sense are these results of obedience or disobedience true for Christians? (You might find Galatians 6:7-10 helpful.)*

**Consider:** What changes of attitude or action have you made in response to things you have read in the Bible? (You may find it helpful to look back over previous notes, and think about what you learnt.) Pray that you will be able to take God's word as seriously as Josiah did.

# 3 The temple sermon

## Jeremiah 7:1-15

Jeremiah 26 gives an account of how this sermon was preached, and the reactions it provoked (read that too if you have time). It was delivered early in the reign of Jehoiakim (26:1) and so not long after the death of Josiah.

Shiloh

**Notes:** 7:12. Shiloh was a place where God was worshipped before the temple was built in Jerusalem. It had been destroyed by the Philistines.

Kinsmen

7:15. A reference to the destruction of the Northern Kingdom, Israel, in the previous century.

From this chapter, and what you read in 2 Kings 22 and 23, think about the effects of Josiah's reforms:

**1** *What had been achieved?*

**2** *From Jeremiah's denunciations here, where had the reforms fallen short?*

It was popularly thought that God would not allow his temple and those who worshipped in it to be destroyed, because of his reputation — if the temple were destroyed it would be assumed that the god of the conquering nation was more powerful than the Lord. However this reasoning was false — God's reputation could also be damaged by the conduct of his worshippers, as we see here.

# The potter

## Jeremiah 18:1-17

This must be one of the most famous incidents in the book! Like the temple sermon, it comes from the early years of Jehoiakim's reign. A potter at work must have been a familiar sight, and the image here is of a pot which doesn't come out quite as intended, so the potter squashes it back down into a lump of clay, and then makes it into something different.

**Read** the passage — more than once — trying to work out how the analogy works. In what sense is the house of Israel like the clay?

**1** *What are God's plans for his people at that moment? Which alternative applies to them (verses 7-10)?*

**2** *What attitude did the people of Israel take? What specific things mentioned here show their lack of repentance?*

**3** *If the people do not repent, what will be the result? There is a sense in which even in this case Jeremiah sees a future for the nation — God can remake the pot. But how far is this a message of hope, how much is it a solemn warning?*

**4** *The temple sermon showed the dilemma between God's plan of blessing his people and their response (or lack of it) to him. How does this passage help us to understand this problem?*

**Consider:** Israel did not repent, so for them this message was a solemn warning. What would you say to someone in the opposite situation, who feels they have failed God, and there is no hope for them? Pray for any who might be in this state.

# 5 The international scene

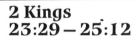

**2 Kings 23:29 – 25:12**

**Read** the passage, and fill in the remaining kings on your time-chart.

The international power-struggles described here are amazingly complex! Assyria had been the dominant power, with Egypt as her nearest rival. Her power had waned, however, and Babylon had come on the scene as a strong contender. 23:29 describes an alliance between the former rivals, Egypt and Assyria, against Babylon. Babylon, however, eventually came out on top, leaving Egypt with still a little influence, and Assyria's power virtually non-existent. Judah, as a tiny state caught in the middle of this, was at Babylon's mercy.

We might attribute Judah's downfall to the power struggle going on around her, and to unwise political decisions at home (*e.g.* 24:1)

**1** *What explanation is given here?*

**2** *Do these two explanations conflict? If not, can you explain why not?*

**3** *What do we learn here about how God works out his purposes in history?*

**Pray:** It is often easier to see what God is doing in the world when you look back, particularly in the history of Israel with her unique position as God's people. The conflicts and power struggles going on in the world today may make little sense. Pray for the trouble-spots which are in the news at the moment in the light of what you have learnt from this passage.

**For the weekend:** In this series of studies, we are concentrating on the history of the times in which Jeremiah lived. The book, however, also contains fascinating glimpses of him as a person, particularly his prayers, as he struggles with the task God has given him. Already you have learnt a bit about Jeremiah from chapter 1 — see what else you can learn about him from 11:14 – 12:6 and 20:7-18. (Some other passages you could look at: 7:16-20,27-34; 8:18 – 9:1; 10:23-25; 14:13-18; 15:10-21; 17:14-18; 18:18-23.)

# Jeremiah, continued

## The scroll

**1**

### Jeremiah 36

This chapter gives us a fascinating glimpse of how some of Jeremiah's prophecies came to be written down. The scroll was probably the first stage in the compilation of the book of Jeremiah as we now have it.

Note the timing of this incident (verses 1 and 9), probably soon after the temple sermon, which may explain why Jeremiah was banned from the temple (verse 5). The fourth year of Jehoiakim (605/604 BC) was shortly after the Egyptians had been decisively beaten by the Babylonians at the Battle of Carchemish, and the fast (verse 9) may have been in response to national danger, as Babylon had just defeated one of Judah's neighbours, Ashkelon.

*Baruch, a close associate of Jeremiah. See - 32:12-16; 43:3-6; 45*

1 *What can you find out from this chapter about the contents of the scroll? What was its basic message?*

2 *Look at how the different characters in the chapter reacted to the message. If you were a political commentator, how would you describe the political situation in Judah? (The officials in verses 10-12 were important ones — the contemporary equivalent of cabinet ministers.) You might try writing a newspaper article assessing the situation.*

*v.23. Scrolls were written sideways, in vertical columns*

**Consider:** We see here some more examples of people's reactions to God's word. How do they compare with Josiah's (Week 7, Study 2)? Has what you learnt then affected your attitude to subsequent studies?

# 2 The letter to the exiles

## Jeremiah 29:1-32

This letter, and the response to it (verses 24-32), perhaps came from the fourth year of Zedekiah's reign (594/593BC). Some of the people were in exile in Babylon, and this letter may have followed a period of unrest among them.

*Jeconiah*

*Figs*

**Note:** *Verse 2.* Jeconiah (RSV) is another name for Jehoiachin. *Verse 17.* The reference to figs comes from Jeremiah's oracle in chapter 24, about God's plan for the exiles, and those who remained in Jerusalem.

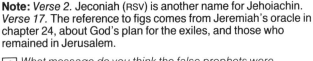

1 *What message do you think the false prophets were preaching to the exiles?*

2 *Why were the people likely to believe them, rather than Jeremiah?*

3 *What aspects of Jeremiah's message do you think the exiles would have found unexpected? (Remember that the Jews thought that the Lord hearing their prayers was associated with the functioning of the temple and the sacrificial system in Jerusalem.)*

**Consider:** The exiles must have felt very confused as they tried to work out God's purposes for them in the middle of what was going on. Have you ever known such a confusing situation? How did things work out? What can you learn to help you cope with such situations in the future? You may find Romans 8:28 a helpful verse to meditate on and memorize as you consider this.

# Hope for the future

## 3

### Jeremiah 31:23-40

Chapters 30 and 31 contain a collection of sayings about Israel's hope for the future and probably originally circulated as a separate scroll (perhaps with chapters 32 and 33 as well) — a Book of Comfort.

*Book of Comfort*

As you read the passage, try to put yourself in the position of the exiles in Babylon, and think how they would have reacted to these promises.

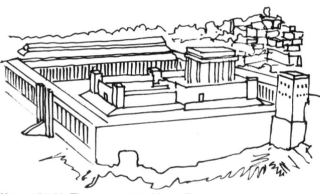

**Notes:** 31:23. The mountain is Mount Zion, where the temple stood in Jerusalem.

*Notes*

31:29. This popular saying probably reflects a feeling among the exiles that they were being punished unjustly for the sins of their ancestors.

**1** *What promises does God make here?*

**2** *How can the Israelites be sure the promises will be kept?*

**3** *How many differences can you find between the old form of religion (its worst forms were denounced by Jeremiah in chapter 7) and the new covenant promised here (verse 31)?*

The concept of the new covenant is very important in the New Testament. It appears in the words of institution at the Last Supper (Luke 22:20; 1 Corinthians 11:25) and the concept is used elsewhere by Paul (*e.g.* 2 Corinthians 3:6). This passage from Jeremiah is quoted by the writer to the Hebrews (8:10-12; 10:16-17) in his argument to show that Jesus has brought about a new state of affairs in man's relationship with God.

# 4 Jerusalem under siege

## Jeremiah 37-38

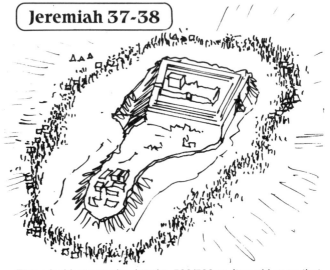

37:12. Perhaps a field Jeremiah bought. See - 32:1-15

38:10. Probably 'three men', not 'thirty' (some translations)

These incidents can be dated to 589/588 BC. It would seem that Zedekiah, although installed as a puppet-king by Nebuchadnezzar, had rebelled against his masters (see 2 Kings 24:20) and that in consequence the Babylonians (Chaldeans, RSV) had laid siege to Jerusalem. Chapter 37 begins with a lull in the siege, caused by an Egyptian army moving towards the city. Imagine the feelings of joy and relief! Jeremiah, however, had the job of telling people that this is not the end of the matter — the Babylonians will return to the attack — and by the time we get to 37:17 it seems that the siege has been resumed.

1 What can you learn about Zedekiah's character from these chapters? What factors affected his political judgments?

2 What do you learn about Jeremiah's character from the way he copes with opposition? (NB. The officials who are hostile to him are different from those in chapter 36, who were presumably by now in exile in Babylon.)

3 Compare this with what you learnt about Jeremiah in Week 7, Study 1. How has his character developed during his ministry?

**Consider:** Jeremiah's strength of character is a tribute to God keeping his promises (1:17-19). That did not mean, however, that he found life easy, as we see in these chapters. What evidence can you find of God's faithfulness in your own life at the moment?

## Jeremiah 39:1 – 40:6

The event which Jeremiah had first prophesied forty years previously (1:13-16) finally happened. Jerusalem fell to the Babylonians and became subject to their rule (39:3 describes the setting-up of a military government). We have read already a fuller account of this in 2 Kings 25:1-12 (repeated in substantially the same form in Jeremiah 52, as a postscript to the book).

**1** *Look back to Week 7, Study 5 and see what you found out about the causes of Judah's downfall. Do you want to add anything in the light of your subsequent reading?*

**2** *In the general judgment which was coming on Judah, the exiles had complained that some of them were being punished unjustly (Jeremiah 31:29-30). How does the example of Ebed-Melech (39:15-18) and indeed Jeremiah himself help to understand what was happening? (How had Ebed-Melech shown his trust in God (39:18)?)*

**3** *Presumably Jeremiah was treated kindly because he was thought to be a friend to Babylon. From this passage, and from your previous reading, what do you think his attitude was to his own country?*

**Consider:** The popular definition of a prophet is someone who foretells the future. How far does Jeremiah fit this definition? Look up 'prophet' in a good Bible Dictionary to see all the main features.

**For the weekend:** There is plenty more of the book for you to read! If you read on, you will find out what happened to Jeremiah in the confused situation in Judah after the fall of Jerusalem. This is followed by a collection of oracles to foreign nations (chapters 46-51) from different points in Jeremiah's career. Alternatively, you can go back and fill in some of the bits we skipped over. As you read, remember that the material is not in chronological order, and look out for any indicatiions of when particular prophecies or incidents are to be dated.

# Human Beings — Warts and All!

## 1 ) Human nature as it was meant to be

### Genesis 1:26-31; Psalm 8

Read these two sections. Then see what they say about each of the following descriptions of human nature. Write the relevant verse(s) beside each statement.

A person in his nature is:-

- deliberately created, the climax of God's creativity
- made in God's image
- enabled to communicate with God
- a sexual being
- made for human companionship
- God's representative on earth to exercise lordship over the rest of creation
- a pleasure to God, evoking his care
- given a purpose in living

*Rushing waterfalls, majestic mountains and delicate flowers cause us to marvel at God's creativity. But if a person is the climax of all creation, he or she is more precious to God than all these. After all, he or she alone can communicate with God. As Jesus said, 'Look at the birds of the air... your heavenly Father feeds them. Are you not much more valuable then they?' (Matthew 6:26). Since humans have such a privileged position, what responsibility does that place upon them? (E.g. treating every person as someone, like you, made in God's image, ensuring that God's world is not spoilt.)*

Praise God for his world and for his care of you in that world. Pray that you will take seriously your responsibility towards it.

# Human nature corrupted 2

## Genesis 3

1 God had made human nature perfect, but the serpent in Genesis 3 argued that it had serious limitations. What were these?

2 The serpent's powers of persuasion won the day. Take each of the statements made in the last study and note down how each of these aspects of human nature was affected by the fall. As with Adam and Eve, so with all of us. Think about how these particular elements of corrupted human nature are present in your own life.

3 But all was not lost. How did God respond to this corruption?

4 Read the commentary on Psalm 8 found in Hebrews 2:5-11. What grounds for hope are to be found there?

5 You may be acutely aware of your own fallen nature. In the light of Hebrews 2 how are you to view your imperfection? Think of what it cost Jesus to make you holy and the fact that he has made you so and in the future will do even more.

In your prayer time, concentrate on Jesus, the perfect man, whose body suffered corruption and who tasted death for everyone so that we might have a new nature. Praise God for him.

# 3 — Fallen nature has far-reaching consequences

> **Ephesians 2:13;**
> **Romans 1:18-32**

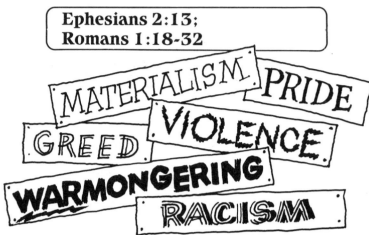

MATERIALISM PRIDE GREED VIOLENCE WARMONGERING RACISM

These two passages contain a vivid description of what the fallen world is like. Write down a summary of what the passages say about our fallen world.

> **1** *We have already seen that Adam and Eve's sin affected their own relationships. But it also led to the corruption of the world and society itself. As you look at the world we live in, how true are Paul's descriptions in his letters to the Ephesians and Romans? E.g. you could think about family relationships, law and order, public honesty. What can people do about it?*

Again we should not despair, for God is still making the truth about himself plain to people.

> **2** *Think of two aspects of society which you are particularly interested in, e.g. education, family life, national politics — all of which reflect the distortion (on some level) of our world from what God intends. Then pray specifically that God's way and righteousness will be revealed here, bringing about change in our world. You could challenge members of your Bible Study group or fellowship to do the same.*

How far would these verses help you to answer a non-Christian who came out with a statement similar to the one Lenin made in 1919? Lenin said: 'The workers are building the new society without having turned themselves into new men who would be free from the dirt of the old world. They are still in it up to their knees.'

Romans 8:1-17

1. *Divide a piece of paper in half lengthways. On one side write down what Paul says about the sinful nature. On the other write down how he describes the new nature. The contrast is startling.*

2. *Now go through the passage again, noticing all that God has done. It is his initiative all the time. Only he can make anyone righteous. The privileges of being a co-heir with Christ are enormous. Take each of the privileges that you have found in this part of the letter and turn them into praise. God has given us guidance for living which we must strive to observe. (We shall look at these in the next Study.)*

He also wants us to relax in him, knowing that we have been given his Spirit so that his righteous demands might be fully met in us.

# 5 My new nature

## Colossians 3:1-17

Although every Christian has a new nature and status, we are all aware that the old nature is still fighting for a survival — a survival which, we are assured, it will never achieve. Paul told the Colossians that they must resist every attempt of the old nature to rear its ugly head.

1 *Read this part of his letter to the Colossian church. Then, put in your own words what he says it means in practice to 'set your mind on things above', both in terms of what things are to be deliberately excluded and what things are to be consciously included in our lives. Pause to assess your own life by these standards of behaviour. Notice that Paul is talking mainly about attitudes.*

2 *Glance back at Romans 8:12-14 to see how Paul puts it another way. Pray that God will help you to put to death what is wrong in your life.*

3 *Paul was not just writing to individuals but to a church. They were to help each other to resist the claims of the old nature. In what ways recently have you helped another Christian to exercise the qualities of a restored nature?*

Think of some way in which this week you will be able to help another Christian to live a holy life, the kind of life God expects from someone whose fallen nature has been restored. Remember however that we do not do this in our own strength. God's Spirit within us is working to make us like Jesus, who came to show us what perfect human nature was meant to be.

**Weekend review**
Over the weekend look back over your notes to trace the progression of human nature. Then read Romans 5-8 in one sitting. This summarizes what God has done in restoring our nature.

# 1 and 2 Timothy; Titus

## Beginning the Pastoral Letters

These Epistles (1 and 2 Timothy and Titus) are so called because they have more to do with the practicalities of church life than the other letters of Paul. They are basically letters to individuals, rather than to a congregation (although they may have been read publicly) and all three deal with similar problems.

   The aim of this study is to get an overall grasp of the contents of these letters. (You can go back and work at the difficult bits later, once you see where they fit in to the whole letter). First of all, the study will work at 1 Timothy, and then you can look at the other two on your own. We shall be looking particularly at three themes, how we can serve God in his church, the problems caused by false teachers, and then at the practical teaching on the life of the church.

## 1 Timothy — a bird's-eye view

**1**

### 1 Timothy

Timothy has been told by Paul to stay in Ephesus (1:3) and has been given a specific job to do there (1:18). It seems that Paul is writing to encourage him and give him some practical help with this job.

**Read** the whole letter (fairly quickly — don't let yourself get bogged down with any difficult bits — you can sort them out later). As you do, make a list of the particular areas of church life Paul wants Timothy to deal with.

*What can you find out about the activities of this church?*

*What were the particular problems it faced?*

**Pray** for your own church — for its regular activities, for those who lead it and for any particular problems it faces at the moment.

# 2 The qualifications for Christian service

## 1 Timothy 1:12-20; 3

**1** *Read* 1:12-20, *where Paul is talking about his own ministry, in contrast to that of the false teachers (1:3-11). What qualifications does Paul have for his job?*

**2** *Read chapter 3. What qualities is Timothy to look for in those he appoints to leadership roles in the church? Some of these probably don't apply to your situation. Can you think of equivalent qualifications which would apply?*

**Consider:** All Christians are called to serve God in some way. How many of these qualifications do you have already? Are there any areas in which you ought to take some action? What are you doing with the qualifications you have got? Take time to pray for those areas of Christian service in which you are already involved (and remember that service for God is not necessarily equivalent to an official title in church or other Christian groups) and also perhaps to ask God if there is anything different he wants you to be involved with. Remember — since gifts are given for the upbuilding of the church, other people are usually better than you at spotting your talents and hidden abilities — ought you to ask someone else for some honest advice?

1 Timothy 4:6 - 5:2; 6:11-21

[1] *What advice does Paul give Timothy about his personal spiritual life?*

[2] *What public duties does Paul give Timothy, both here and in the rest of the letter? (Look back to Study 1!)*

[3] *In what ways will the state of Timothy's spiritual life affect his public duties?*

**Consider:** The personal application should be obvious! Look again at Paul's advice on Timothy's spiritual life, and try to translate it into practical terms for your own situation.

As you come to pray, pray not only for yourself, but also for the personal spiritual life of Christian leaders you know.

# 4 False teaching in the church

## 1 Timothy 1:3-11; 4:1-5; 6:3-10

One of the problems which was very common in the early church was that of people who came into the church teaching variations of the apostolic teaching, often with a Jewish slant.

**Read** the passages which deal with this subject (1:3-11; 4:1-5; 6:3-10) and from them make a list of contrasts between true and false teaching (perhaps in two columns in your notebook).

1 *How did Timothy know what was true teaching? (There's a lot more on this in 2 Timothy — look out for it there.)*

2 *Can you think of any forms of false teaching which are commonly found today, either within the church or outside it? Can you find anything here to help in knowing how to deal with it?*

If one of the sects — such as the Jehovah's Witnesses, or the Moonies — is common in your area, it would be worth finding out a bit about it. Perhaps read a book on the subject, such as *The Challenge of the Cults* (by M. C. Burrell — on recent cults), *Some Modern Faiths* (Burrell/Wright) and *The Rising of the Moon* (John Allan — on the Moonies) — all published by IVP.

# The life of the church

## 5

### 1 Timothy 2:1-10; 5:3-16

These Epistles do not give us a 'blue-print' for church life; they are mainly concerned to correct things that were going wrong. You may be able to think of other areas for concern in the life of your church, but it's worth looking at the things Paul picks up to see if they need some attention as well.

*The church's prayer 2:1-10*

**1** *What is the church to pray for, and why?*

**2** *How is the church to pray? What is the relevance here of instruction on the way they live?*

**Consider:** What is the scope of the prayer of your church or other Christian group. Is it as wide as Paul envisages here? If not, what practical steps could you take to encourage a wider interest? (And what about your own praying?)

The financial needs of widows in the first century may seem remote to us, especially with the welfare state to care for those who have no other means of support.

*Practical needs 5:3-16*

**3** *What does Paul say here is the responsibility of individual Christians, rather than the church as a whole?*

**4** *Do you think the church has a continuing responsibility in this area? If so, what are the equivalent needs? How might they be met?*

### Weekend work project
Now go on to look at the other two Pastoral Epistles (2 Timothy and Titus) on your own. You may find it helpful to continue looking at our three themes — start by reading a whole Epistle and noting sections which apply to these themes, and also any other subjects which occur. Then you can go back and work on bits of particular interest in more detail.

# Time with God

1. Find a time when you can be alone and undisturbed. Most people find that the morning is best.

2. Consciously make an effort to slow down and be quiet. Think about the God you are coming to and be prepared to talk to him — about himself, yourself and the time that you will spend together.

3. Read the Bible passage for the day — preferably more than once unless it's very long. Try to get a clear picture of what it is about by careful reading. What does it teach me for or about today?

4. Have a notebook handy and write down your thoughts.

5. Now is the time to use the workbook. Don't cheat by letting it do your thinking for you. It is a good principle to learn and then to act upon what you have learnt.

6. Spend some time talking to God — praising him, thanking him, bringing personal and wider concerns to him, asking him to help you really to *learn* and *act upon* what you have understood from the Bible today.

7. Finally, be ready for anything that God particularly wants to tell you for, or about, today. Be prepared to commit yourself honestly in response.

# Further Reading from IVP

## Bible reference books
*The book that Jesus read.* Geoff Treasure re-tells the Old Testament story for those who have never managed to 'get into' it. Pocketbook, 128 pages.

*Pocket guide to the Old Testament.* A handy introduction for those wanting to study the Old Testament. Cyril Bridgland. Pocketbook, 240 pages.

*Pocket guide to the New Testament.* A pocket work of reference for the New Testament. Each book is described with sections on the authorship, date, purpose and a brief summary of the contents. Francis Foulkes. Pocketbook, 160 pages.

*The New Testament documents.* This book asks and answers the questions: Are the New Testament documents reliable? Can we have confidence in the historicity of the facts which they record? F. F. Bruce. Pocketbook, 128 pages.

*New Bible Dictionary or Illustrated Bible Dictionary.* An A to Z of Bible terms and concepts by over 150 scholars. Available either in one volume, text only edition or as the three volume *Illustrated Bible Dictionary* with nearly 2000 photographs, diagrams and maps. General editor Norman Hillyer.


## Books for Bible study
*Search the Scriptures.* Edited by Alan M. Stibbs, a systematic course of daily study, designed to cover the whole Bible in three years. Paperback, 496 pages.

*Tyndale Commentaries.* This excellent series is designed to help the ordinary Bible reader understand what the text actually says and what it means. Covers all the New Testament and a large portion of the Old Testament. Paperback.

*New Bible Commentary.* Edited by Donald Guthrie and others. Probably the best one-volume commentary on the whole Bible at present available in the English language. Hardback, 1310 pages.

## Bible teaching
*Know the Truth.* A handbook of Christian belief to help Christians grasp the overall pattern of the Bible's teaching. This readable study book provides lots of Scripture references and discussion questions. Bruce Milne. Paperback, 288 pages.

## LET US HELP YOU TO HELP YOUR FRIENDS

We hope you have enjoyed using *Know your Bible.* We would like to help you go on to further workbooks in this series and encourage others to benefit from them. We are therefore offering two voucher schemes for you or your church members to use:-

# FREE COPY

Use this voucher to claim your free copy of a *Know your Bible* workbook when you purchase 10 or more copies at one time for your group Bible study or for church members.

## TO THE BOOKSELLER

IVP will replace the workbook given to the customer when this voucher is presented at the single purchase of 10 or more copies of a *Know your Bible* workbook.

Please indicate which volume is to be replaced: _____

This offer finishes 30th June 1986 and is applicable only to the UK. Send this voucher to IVP, Norton Street, Nottingham NG7 3HR.

Name and address of purchaser:

Bookshop stamp

KNOW YOUR BIBLE

# 30p off

### KNOW YOUR BIBLE WORKBOOKS

Bookshop stamp

Use this voucher when you purchase any workbook (excluding Nos. 1 & 2) in the *Know your Bible* series.

Only one voucher per workbook purchased

## TO THE BOOKSELLER

IVP will redeem this voucher for 30p when used in the purchase of a *Know your Bible* workbook (excluding Nos. 1 & 2)

Please send it to IVP, Norton Street, Nottingham NG7 3HR

Offer finishes 30th June 1986 and is applicable to UK only.

KNOW YOUR BIBLE